All About Dinosaurs

Tyrannosaurus Rex

Daniel Nunn

Raintree is an imprint of Capstone Global Library Limited, a company incorporated in England and Wales having its registered office at 7 Pilgrim Street, London, EC4V 6LB – Registered company number: 6695582

www.raintreepublishers.co.uk
myorders@raintreepublishers.co.uk

Text © Capstone Global Library Limited 2015
The moral rights of the proprietor have been asserted.

Edited by Daniel Nunn and James Benefield
Designed by Tim Bond
Picture research by Tracy Cummins
Production by Helen McCreath
Originated by Capstone Global Library Ltd
Printed and bound in China

ISBN 978 1 4062 8088 3
18 17 16 15 14
10 9 8 7 6 5 4 3 2 1

British Library Cataloguing in Publication Data
A full catalogue record for this book is available from the British Library.

Acknowledgements
We would like to thank the following for permission to reproduce photographs: Getty Images pp. 9 (ROGER HARRIS), 17 (Jay P. Morgan), 18, 23 (Richard Nowitz); Science Source pp. 4 (José Antonio Peñas), 20 (Harold Brodrick); Shutterstock pp. 5a, 13 (DM7), 5b (Maria Dryfhout), 5c (Karen Givens), 5d, 23 (Piotr Gatlik), 7 bottom (Svinkin), 7 top (Sofia Santos), 8 (Elenarts), 10, 12 (TsuneoMP), 11, 14 (Bob Orsillo), 16 (MaksiMages), 19 (hans engbers); Superstock pp. 6 (NHPA), 15 (Stocktrek Images), 21 (Tips Images).

Cover photograph of Tyrannosaurus rex, reproduced with permission of Getty Images (ROGER HARRIS/SPL).

Back cover photograph of Tyrannosaurus rex reproduced with permission of Shutterstock (Elenarts).

We would like to thank Dee Reid and Nancy Harris for their invaluable help in the preparation of this book.

Every effort has been made to contact copyright holders of material reproduced in this book. Any omissions will be rectified in subsequent printings if notice is given to the publisher.

Contents

Meet Tyrannosaurus rex

Tyrannosaurus rex was a dinosaur.
Dinosaurs lived long ago.

dinosaur

snake

crocodile

lizard

Dinosaurs were reptiles.
Snakes, crocodiles and lizards
are reptiles that live today.

5

What was Tyrannosaurus rex like?

Tyrannosaurus rex was a very big dinosaur.

Tyrannosaurus rex was longer than a bus!

Tyrannosaurus rex had strong
back legs.

Tyrannosaurus rex was fast.

Tyrannosaurus rex had a long tail.

Tyrannosaurus rex's tail stopped it from falling over.

arms

Tyrannosaurus rex had short arms.

teeth

Tyrannosaurus rex had very sharp teeth.

Tyrannosaurus rex had a strong bite.

Tyrannosaurus rex ate other dinosaurs.

Where is Tyrannosaurus rex now?

Tyrannosaurus rex are extinct. There are no Tyrannosaurs rex alive now.

All the dinosaurs died long ago.

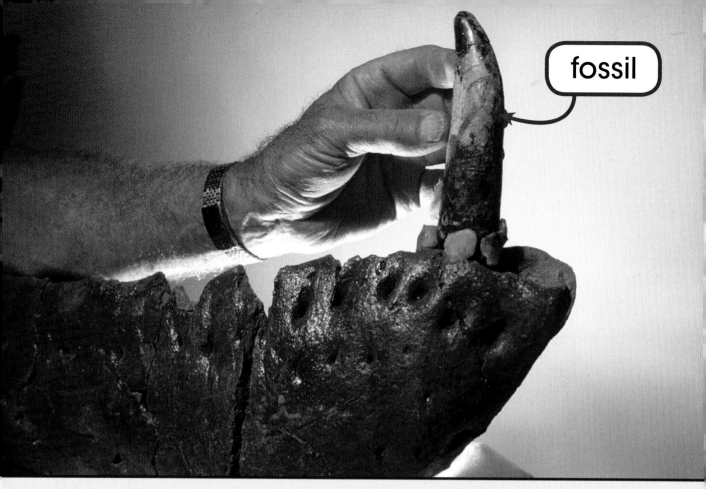

fossil

We learn about Tyrannosaurus rex from fossils.

Fossils are animal bones that have turned to rock.

People find fossils in the ground.

Fossils show us what Tyrannosaurus rex looked like.

Where in the world?

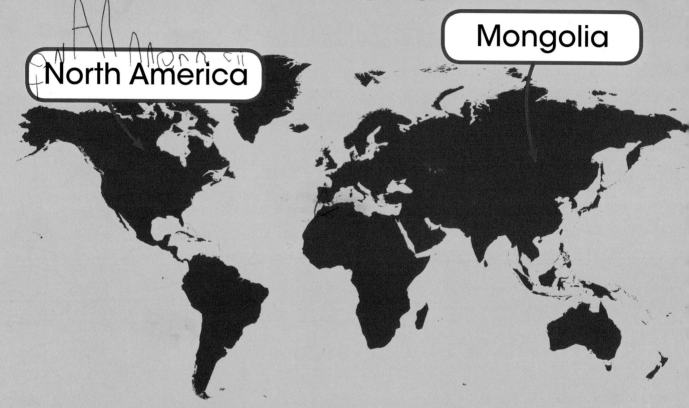

Mongolia

North America

Tyrannosaurus rex fossils have
been found in North America
and Mongolia.

Picture glossary

 **fossil** animal bones or parts of a plant that have turned into rock

 **reptile** cold-blooded animal. A lizard is a reptile.

How to say it

Tyrannosaurus rex: say 'tie-ran-uh-sawr-us rex'

Index

Notes for parents and teachers

Before reading

Ask the children to name some dinosaurs. Ask them if dinosaurs are around today. Talk about how some dinosaurs ate plants and others ate other dinosaurs. Can they think of ways these dinosaurs might have been different? Have they heard of Tyrannosaurus rex? Find out if they already know anything about this dinosaur.

After reading

- Make Tyrannosaurus rex sock puppets. Give each child a sock and ask them to stick eyes on each side of the head and lots of sharp teeth in the mouth. They can add small arms at the front. Get the children to ask their puppet questions about what it was like to be a Tyrannosaurus rex.
- Make Tyrannosaurus rex teeth out of clay. They should be at least as long as a child's hand! Make sure they are sharp and then put the dry 'fossils' in your own museum.